My Family Myself

AF322957

Author and Editor: Carol Batchelor, B.A., M.A.

Illustration and Design: Margaret Horvath

Hayes Publishing Ltd.
3312 Mainway
Burlington, Ontario
L7M 1A7

Copyright© 1983 by Hayes Publishing Ltd. All rights reserved. No part of this work may be reproduced or transmitted in any form or by any means, electronic or mechanical, including photocopying and recording, or by any information storage or retrieval system, without permission in writing from the Publisher.

ISBN 0-88625-043-9

I'm a new branch on our family tree

My Full Name Is: ____

First   Middle   Last

I asked my mother why she named me what she did, and this is what she said:

____

____

____

Where I Live: ____

Number/Street   Apt. or Unit No.

____

Town/City   Province/State

____

Country   Code

My telephone number (plus area code) ______________________

I am __________ years old right now.

ALL ABOUT ME

My Date of Birth:

I was born on the _____________ th day of

(month) _____________ in 19 _____________,

at (hospital or place) _____________

in (city or town) _____________

in (country) _____________

Was there anything unusual about
your birth? Ask your mother.

____

____

____

____

____

When I was born, I weighed_____________
kilograms.

When I was born, I measured _____________
cm long.

I was born with (color) _____________

eyes. I had hair of (color) _____________;
it was (circle the right word) curly,
straight, long, short, wispy, green.

Here is a print (a copy) of my very first

baby picture. I was _____________
days/weeks/months old.

If you don't have a photograph, draw a picture
of what your Mother said you looked like as a
baby. (above)

When I Was Still A Baby

I asked my mother about when I was a baby, and she said, or remembered, or looked up in my baby book, these things:

I got my first tooth at (age in months) _______________.

My first word was _______________,
and I said it at (age) _______________.

I crawled when I was (age) _______________.

I walked when I was (age) _______________.

ABOUT ME RIGHT NOW

Here is some information about me right now:

I stand _______________ cm tall.

I weigh _______________ kg.

I have (color) _______________ eyes.

My hair is _______________ in color and it's (circle the right word) long, straight, curly, short, wavy, frizzy, purple.

I wear size _______________ clothes and

size _______________ shoes.

I have grown _______________ cm in the

last _______________ year(s).

Mark your height on the growth chart.

List some unique things about yourself. For example, have you ever had your tonsils out? Your appendix? Did you ever fall down and break anything? An arm? A leg? Ask your mother if she remembers you doing anything unusual as a small child or baby. Do you have a birth-mark or any scars? (Like where you skinned your knee last week?)

____

____

____

____

____

____

Draw a picture of you and your friend's favorite activity here.

You've got lots of friends, but everybody's got a best friend. Who's yours? ____________________

What type of things do you and your friend do after school and in your spare time? Do you paint? Ride a bike? Take music, swimming or other lessons?

____

____

____

____

____

More about me later; right now let's take a look at the other branches of my family tree. ...

These are My Parents

Father

My Father's Full Name is: ______________

____

He was born on the ______________th day of

(month) ______________,

in the year __________.

Mother

My Mother's Full Name Is: ______________

____

My mother's maiden name was: ______________

(A 'maiden' name is the last name or surname that your mother was born with. When women marry they usually take their new husband's last name; but sometimes they don't, it depends on the person.)

Here are some photographs or drawings of my parents.

My father was born at (hospital or place name) ______________,

in (city/town) ______________

______________,

in country ______________.

When I asked my father about himself at my age (I asked him things like what were his favorite toys, games, friends, places, vacations, TV shows, singers, clubs and movie stars), this is what he said: ______________

____

____

____

Father used to go to ______________ ______________ school.

Mother was born on the ______________ th day of (month) ______________ in the year ______________.

She was born at (hospital or place name) ______________

in (town/city) ______________,

in (country) ______________.

I asked my mother some of the same questions too. This is what she said:

____

____

____

Mother used to go to ______________ ______________ school.

MORE ABOUT MY PARENTS

Here is a print of my parents' wedding photograph, or, a drawing I did, using the information my parents gave me.

When and where my mother and father first met: ___________________

____

____

They dated or knew each other

for ___________ (years/months/weeks) before they were married.

They were married on the ________th

day of (month) _____________ in the

year _________.

They did/did not go on a honeymoon.

If they did, where did they go? ________

____

____

Here's how mother and father described their wedding day:

____

____

____

____

____

If your parents were not born in the country you now live in, state here when they came to this country.

____

These are the jobs my parents have had over the years:

____

____

Here are some photographs or drawings of my brothers and sisters and myself.

These are their names and ages:

___________________________ ______years old

___________________________ ______years old

___________________________ ______years old

___________________________ ______years old

If any of your brothers and sisters don't live at home now, write in below where they do live and why. Or, if any are married, write in to whom they are married, when they got married and the names of their children if they have any.

____

____

____

____

Is there anything unusual about your brothers and sisters? Are any of them astronauts or mad scientists?

____

____

____

Write down the things you like best about your brothers and sisters.

____

____

____

BROTHERS AND SISTERS

What do you think are the things about you that your brothers and sisters like best? ___________________

____

____

____

Tell here what you like about having brothers and sisters. Do you get to borrow their toys? Books? Clothes? Do they play with you when everyone else is busy? OR If you DON'T have any brothers and sisters, write here what you like about being an only child.

____

____

MY FAMILY TREE SO FAR

FATHER'S NAME

MOTHER'S MAIDEN NAME

YOUR NAME

BROTHERS   **SISTERS**

HERE IS OUR HOME 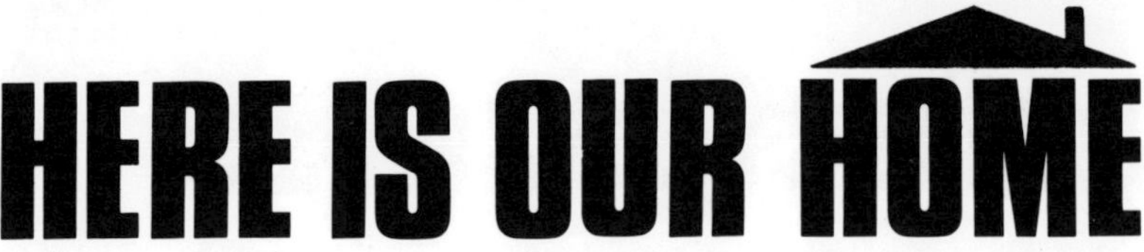 **This is where we all live.**

Do you live in a house? An apartment? A boat? A farm house? A condominium? A balloon? A trailer? A submarine? _______________________________________

Where would you like to live? _______________________________________

What do you like best about your home? _______________________________________

____

Draw a picture of your home.

How many people live in your home with you? (Remember to count yourself!) _______________________

Do you have any animals or pets living with you? _______________. How many? _______________ What kind?

____

____

Do you have your own bedroom? (yes or no) _______ OR do you share a room with someone else? _______ (yes or no)

Who do you share with? _______

____

____

Is your home big or small? _______

How many rooms does it have? _______________________

How many floor levels? Houses usually have more than one, but apartments generally have only one. Which is it in your case?

____

____

Have you always lived here? _______ (yes or no) If not, where have you lived before this house or home?

____

____

____

Addresses: _______________________

____

____

____

When and why you moved: _______

____

____

____

Other schools you've been to: _______

____

____

For what grades? _______________________

Does your family own a car? _______

How many? _______________ What kind?

_______________ How about a van?

_______ A truck? _______ A boat?

_______ A snowmobile? _______

A plane? _______ A spaceship?

Every family has two sides to it, because everyone has a father and a mother. There's your mother's side of the family and your father's side. Each of your parents also has a mother and a father, your grandparents. Your mother's parents are your grandparents and, because they're on your mother's side of the family, they're known as your **maternal grandparents.** ('Maternal' comes from the word 'mother'.) Your father's parents are your **paternal grandparents.** ('Paternal' comes from the root of the word 'father'.)

Now we're going to go back one generation in your family and look at your grandparents. (By the way, 'generation' is a word that means 'the time span separating a parent and a child.' You and your parents are two separate generations. Historians like things to be simple and even, so they say that a generation is 30 years.)

OK, let's get down to business!

PATERNAL GRANDFATHER

Grandfather's Full Name Is: ______

______

He was born on the ______ th day of (month) ______, in (year) ______, in the (city/town) of ______ in (country) ______.

What job(s) did your grandfather have? ______

______

How long did he work at that? ______

______

Ask your father all about your grandfather or, if he's still alive, ask him yourself what life was like when he was growing up. Where did he grow up? What school(s) did he go to? What subjects did he take in school? (You'll be surprised at how different things were then!) What types of food did he eat as a kid? What did he do for entertainment? Sports? Books? Games? TV? Radio? What types of transportation were available to him then? ______

______

Was your grandfather ever in a war? ______ Which one? ______

What did he do? ______

Was there ever an article about him in the newspaper?

If so, why? ______

______

YOUR FATHER'S MOTHER IS YOUR

PATERNAL GRANDMOTHER

Grandmother's Full Name Is:

____

Her maiden name was:___________________

__________________(Remember what a 'maiden' name is?)

She was born on the ________th day of

(month) ____________________in the year

____________________, in the (town/city) of

______________ in (country) _____________.

Ask your grandmother all about her childhood, the things she did, the places she went and why, the friends she had, her favorite foods and how they were made. Find out if you can what schools she went to and what her grades were like. Ask her to describe her favorite party dress to you. Could you draw it for her?

____

____

____

____

When and where did your grandparents meet? ___________________

____

When did they get married?___________

____________________Where?___________

How many children did they have? _______________________________

Their names: ______________________

____

Did your grandmother ever have a job? (yes or no) ____________ If she did, what did she do? _________________

For how long? ___________________

What do you like the very best about your grandmother? ________________

____

____

____

____

Ask your mother what she likes best about her mother.

Put in a photograph or draw a picture of your grandparents.

Now we're going to have a closer look at your mother's side of the family. We'll start with her father, your maternal grandfather.

Grandfather's Full Name Is:

____

He was born on the _______th day of (month) _______
in the year _________, in (city/town) _____________
in (country)___________________________________ .

What was your grandfather's occupation? _________

____

Did he ever change jobs?_________________ Why?

____

You can ask this grandfather all the same types of questions you asked your father's father. What were his grades like in school?

____

____

Ask your mother what she likes best about her father.

____

____

What do you like best about your grandfather?

____

____

What kinds of accomplishments did your grandfather make? Was he a soldier or a sailor or a flyer? Do you have any newspaper clippings of him? Did he ever build or make anything special for you?

____

____

____

Where does your grandfather live? _____________

Do you talk to him on the telephone or write letters to him? What do you talk about?

____

Grandparents are a great source of information on just about anything. Ask your grandparents all the questions you can think of, but remember not to be a bother to them. If you can't talk directly to your grandparents, why not write to them? They'd love to hear from you and they would be very pleased to know that you are interested in the family.

MATERNAL GRANDFATHER

Draw a picture of your grandfather.

If some or all of your grandparents are no longer living, you can still find out general information about their generation by asking other older people that you know (like the older couple down the hall or down the street). And you can get specific information about your own grandparents from your parents and your aunts and uncles.

MATERNAL GRANDMOTHER

Draw a picture of your grandmother.

YOUR MATERNAL GRANDMOTHER IS YOUR
M ______________________'S MOTHER
Grandmother's Full Name Is:

____
The name she was born with or her maiden name
was: ______________________________
She was born in the year______, on the______th
day of (month) ____________________, in (city/town)
__________________, in (country)______________.
Ask your mother all about your grandmother or, if you can, ask her yourself about her girlhood. What was her favorite doll or toy when she was quite young? Did she ever sing in a choir?

____

____

____
Does your grandmother cook any special foods for you?______________ What does she make?

____
When do you get to see your grandmother? ______

____
Where does she live? ______________________
What kind of job(s) has she ever had? __________
__________________ When? ______________
Ask her when she and your grandfather first met.

____
Ask her about their 'courtship'. (That's sort of like dating. What did they do together? Where did they go?

____

____

____
When did she marry your grandfather? __________
Where?________________________________
Was it a big wedding or a small one? __________
Write down some of the special times you've had with your grandmother.

____

____

ROUNDING OUT YOUR PARENTS' GENERATION – YOUR AUNTS AND UNCLES

Just like you may have brothers and sisters, your parents may have brothers and sisters too. These people are your UNCLES and AUNTS, and you are a NIECE (if you're a girl) or a NEPHEW (if you're a boy) to them.

How many aunts and uncles do you have? (Count both sides of the family.)

____

What are their names? (List them here.) _______________________________

____

____

____

Are any of them married? __________
How many? ______________

What are their spouses' names?

____

____

____

The word 'spouse' means either a husband or a wife. Who are these spouses to you? The spouse of your aunt, her husband, is still your uncle, but he is an uncle 'by-marriage', not a direct relative like your aunt.

Do your aunts and uncles live close to you? _______________________(yes or no)

Where do they live? ______________

____

____

____

Do you get to see them often? ______

____

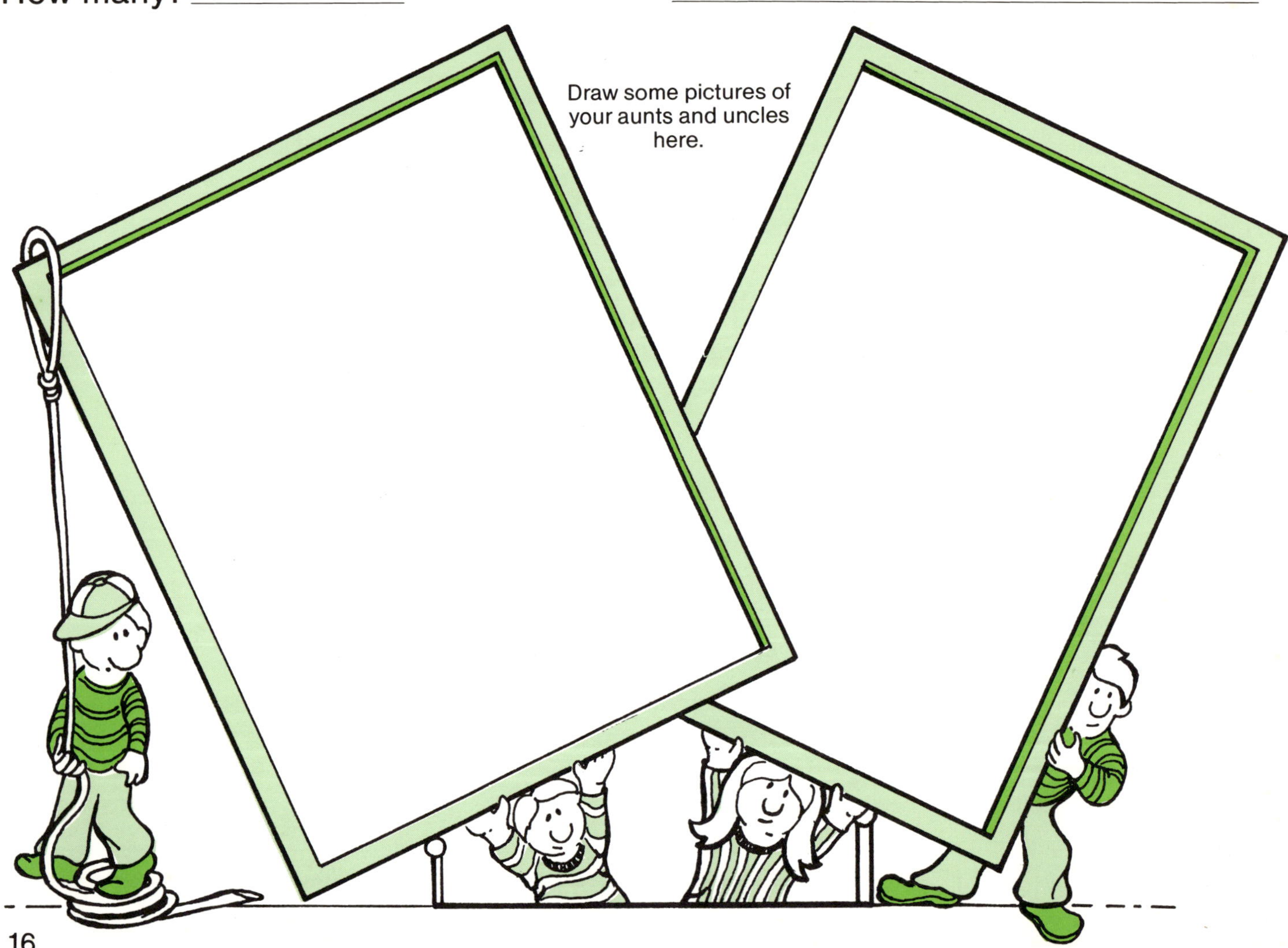

Draw some pictures of your aunts and uncles here.

MY GROWING FAMILY TREE

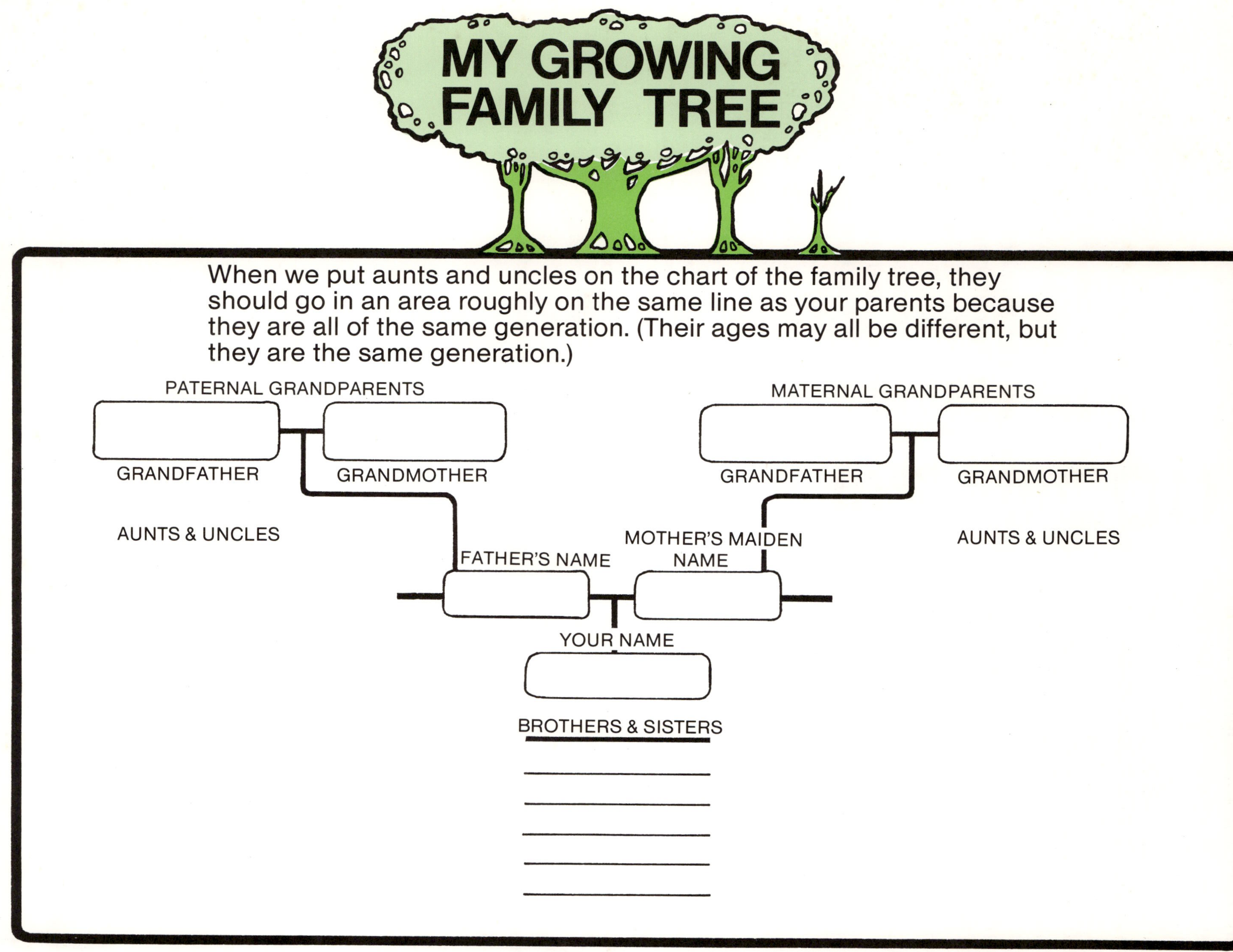

OK, you've got some aunts and some uncles and some or all of them are married. Do any of them have any children? How are these children related to you? They are your COUSINS. (Cousins can be either boys or girls.) And then what are you to them? You're their cousin too. Why? Because just as their mother and father are your aunt and uncle, your mother and father are aunt and uncle to them.

Name all your cousins: (Put in their ages too!) ________________

____

____

____

COUSINS

Let's add your cousins to the chart. Remember, they are of your generation, so they should go in an area roughly in line with you and your brothers and sisters. (The chart may be getting a bit crowded by now, and yours won't look exactly like your friend's down the street, but don't worry, all families are different. Just fit the people in as best you can.)

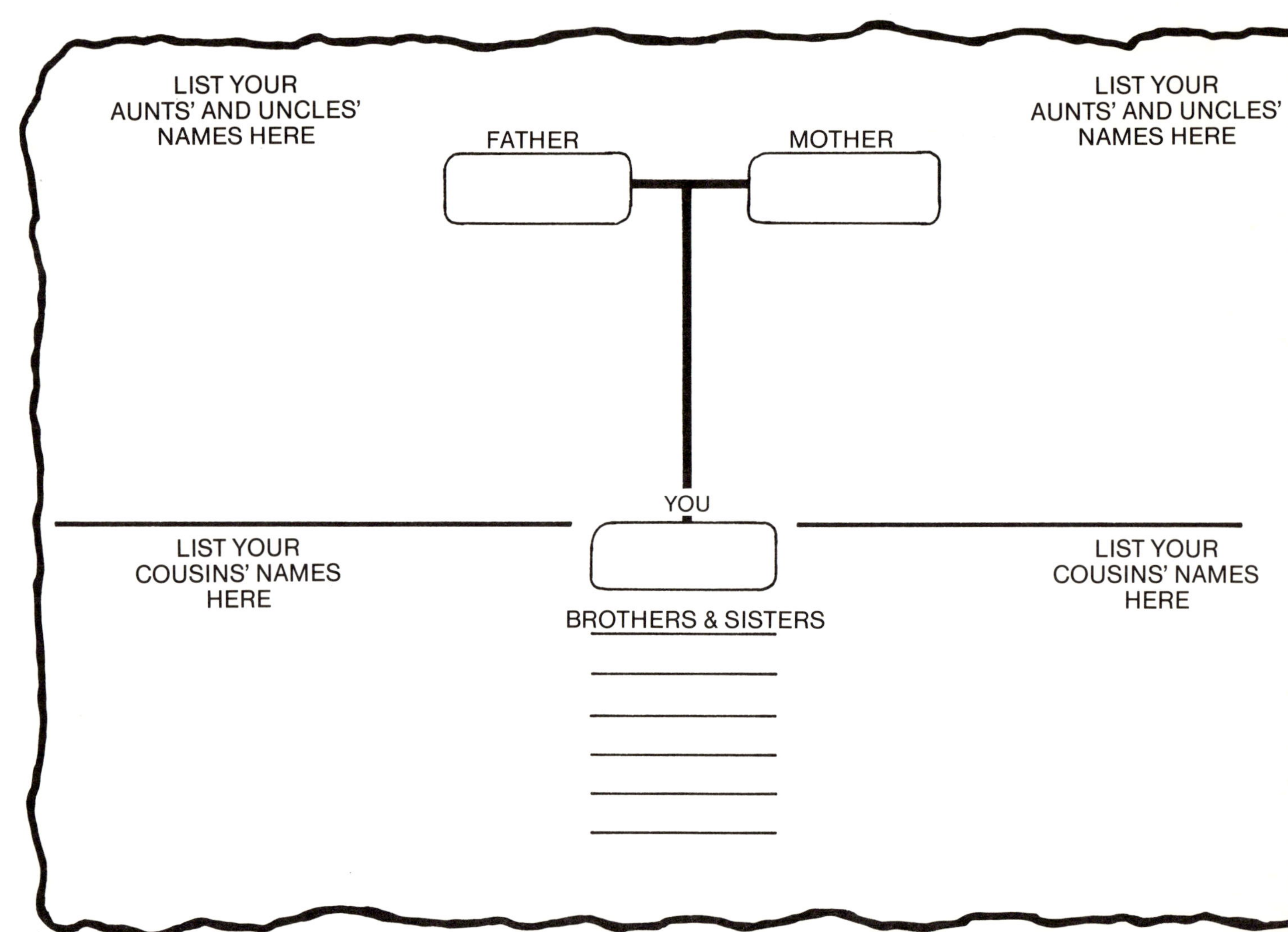

My goodness, there are a lot of people related to you, aren't there?

Does Your Family Have A "SKELETON" In Its Closet?

This means a relative who was different from all the rest, like a 'black sheep.' For example, many generations back your people may all have been very religious and law-abiding people, but an uncle or a cousin may have been a pirate! These folk may not have liked to talk about this family member and he or she may be remembered as a 'skeleton in the closet.'

But don't worry about your unusual relative, almost every family has at least one member who's different from the rest!

Let's start fresh and see if we can get everyone organized properly on a new chart. (You may find it easier to fill in this chart after you've read all of this book.) Think about the number of people you must include in which categories and age ranges before you begin. It might be best to work in pencil so that if you make any mistakes or it gets too crowded, you can erase parts and start over. Have fun!

We are charting your 'ancestors' who are all the people from whom you are descended.

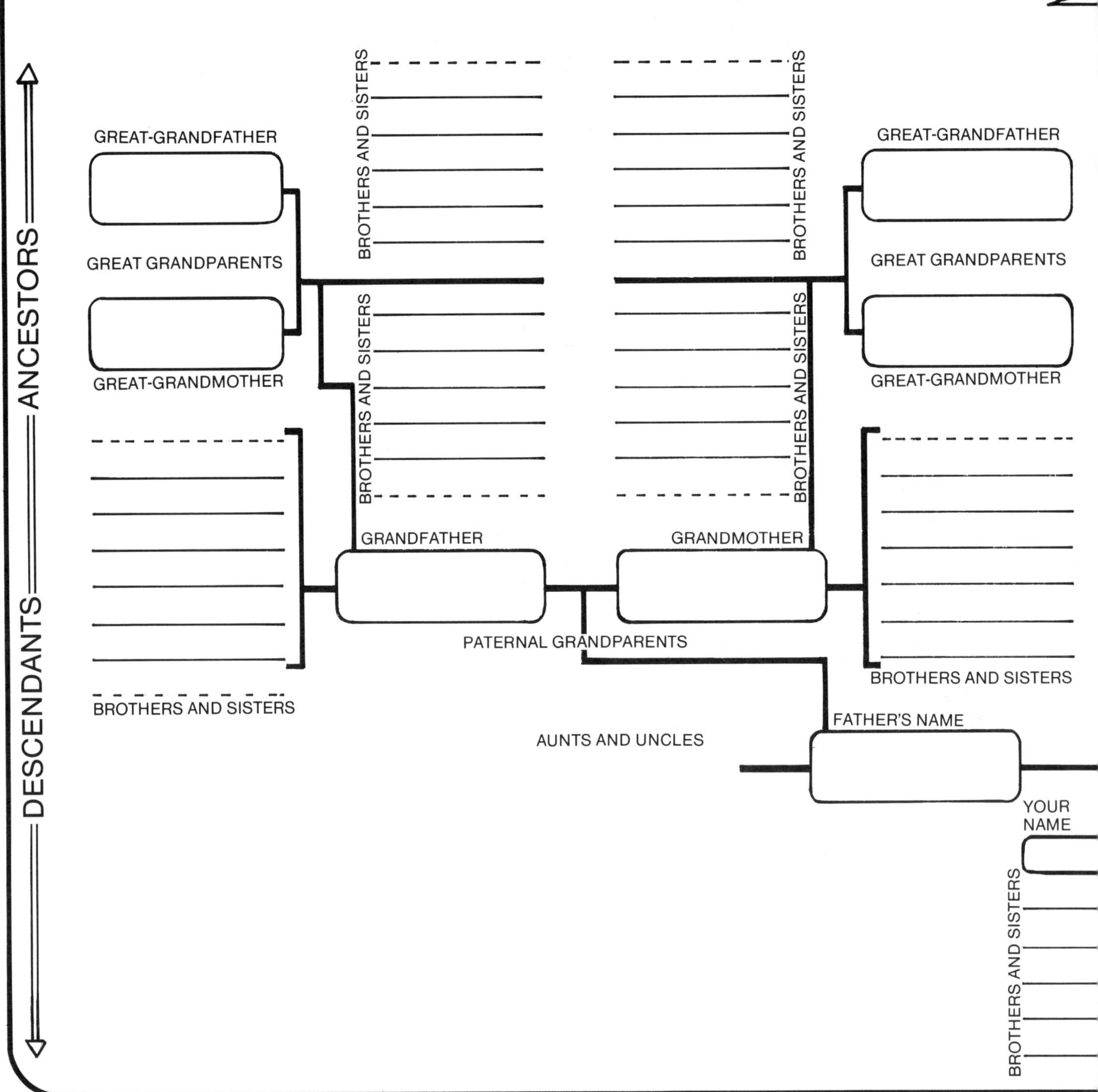

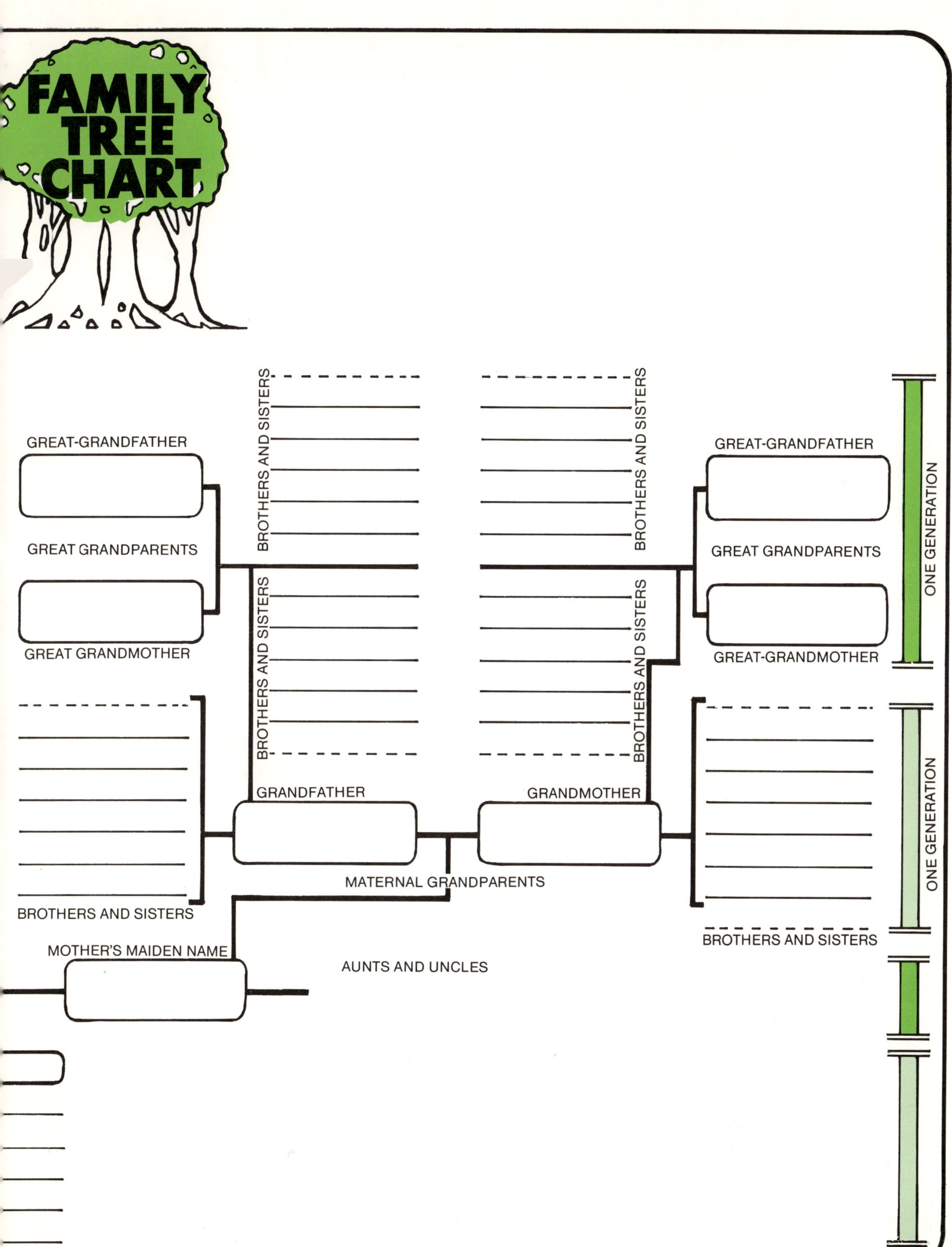

FAMILY TREE CHART
GREAT-GRANDFATHER
GREAT GRANDPARENTS
GREAT GRANDMOTHER
BROTHERS AND SISTERS
BROTHERS AND SISTERS
BROTHERS AND SISTERS
BROTHERS AND SISTERS
GREAT-GRANDFATHER
GREAT GRANDPARENTS
GREAT-GRANDMOTHER
ONE GENERATION
ONE GENERATION
GRANDFATHER
GRANDMOTHER
MATERNAL GRANDPARENTS
BROTHERS AND SISTERS
BROTHERS AND SISTERS
MOTHER'S MAIDEN NAME
AUNTS AND UNCLES

THE "GREATS"

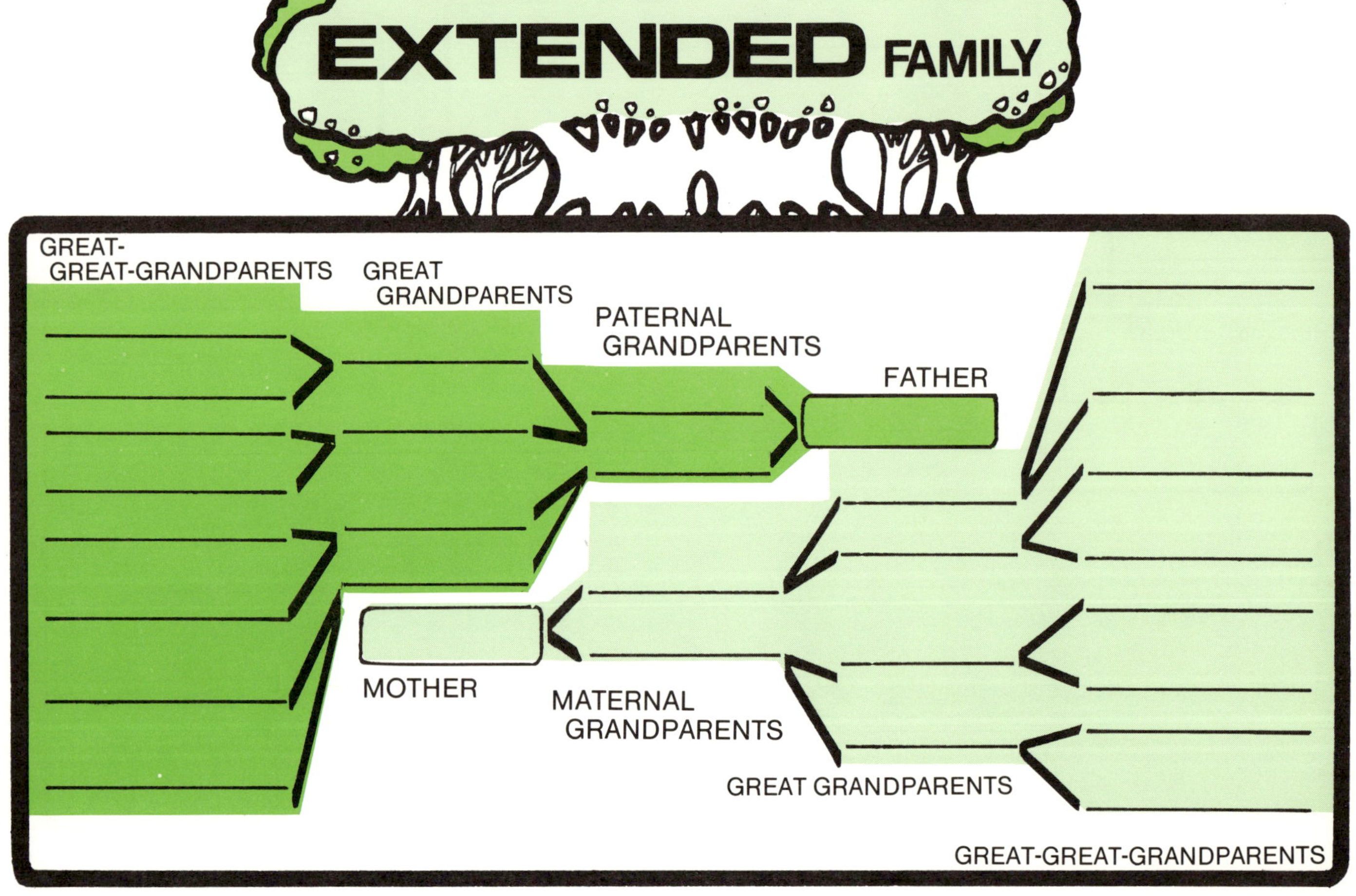

Just as you have 2 sides to your family, and your parents each have 2 sides to their families, your grandparents each have two sides, and so on.

You have 2 parents, 4 grandparents and then 8 great-grandparents. 'Great' used in this way means another generation backwards or removed from you. And you can just keep on going back to great-great-grandparents. It gets complicated, doesn't it? It's easier to show on a chart than it is to talk about it.

Here's a chart. Can your parents help you to fill in your great-grandparents? See how far back you can go.

If this photo was taken 3 generations ago, roughly how long ago was that? How do you think you would color it? Try.

KIN you find your Relatives?

A word search game.

grandfather
relationship
kin
kids
papa
granny
relative
tree
nana
sibling
family
sister
gramps
nephew
grandmother
mom
father
uncle
mother
cousin
great
grandma
dad
parent
brother
aunt
niece
ma

All these words are hidden in the puzzle somewhere. The words can run up or down, forwards or backwards, or diagonally. How many can you find?

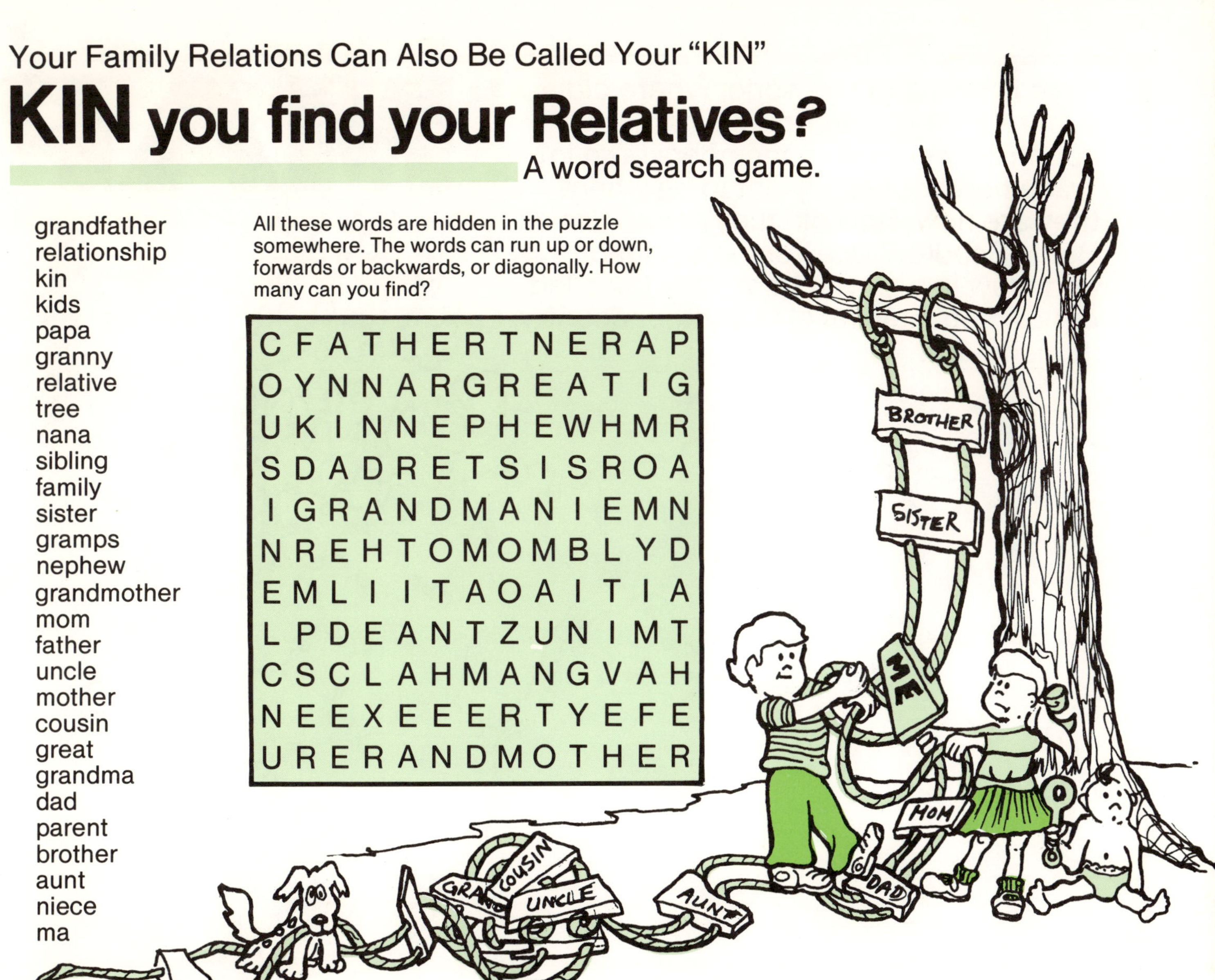

MORE GREATS

Your parents' brothers and sisters are your uncles and aunts, right? Right. Who do you think your grandparents' brothers and sisters are to you? They're your great aunts and great uncles. You, then, would be a 'great' niece or nephew to them. And if your great-grandparents had sisters and brothers, these people would be your great-great aunts and uncles. There are more 'greats' used here to keep straight the number of generations removed from you. Look again and you'll see how the 'grand' in 'grandmother' takes the place of 'great.' Your grandmother could really be called your 'great-mother.'

Are you totally confused yet? Well, let's straighten it out by means of the big chart on Pages 20 and 21. Place your grandparents' brothers and sisters on a level roughly with them.

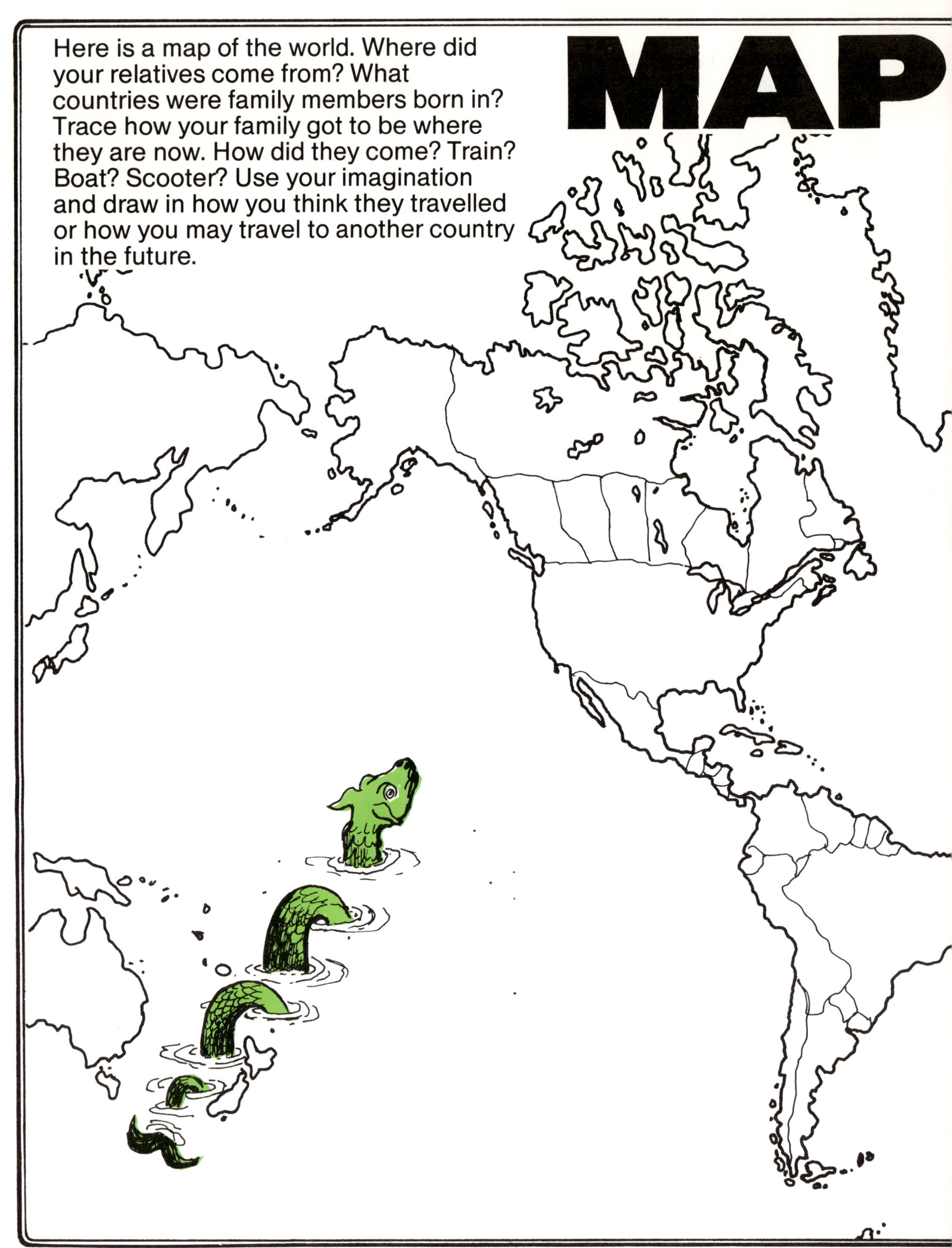

MAP

Here is a map of the world. Where did
your relatives come from? What
countries were family members born in?
Trace how your family got to be where
they are now. How did they come? Train?
Boat? Scooter? Use your imagination
and draw in how you think they travelled
or how you may travel to another country
in the future.

of the
world

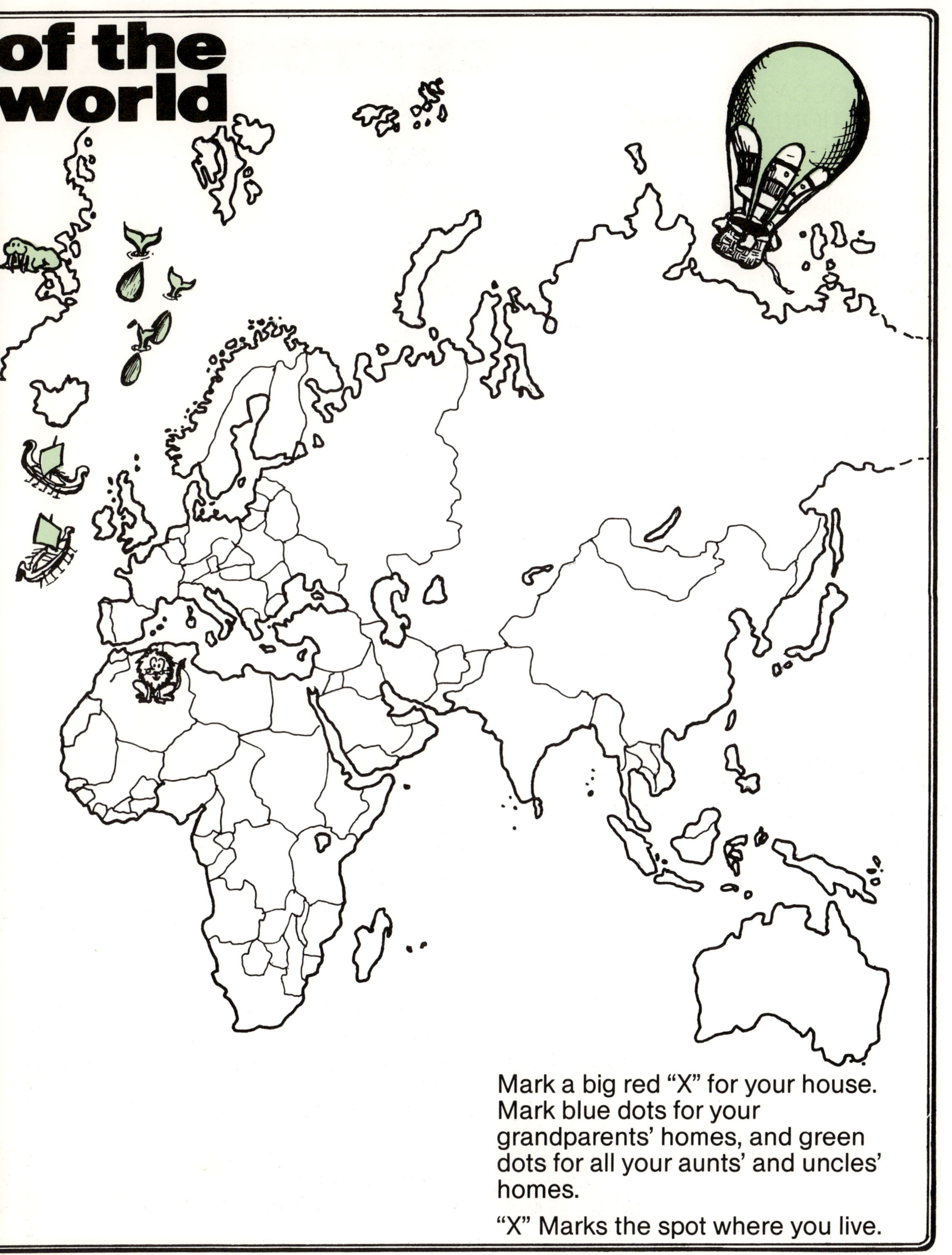

Mark a big red "X" for your house. Mark blue dots for your grandparents' homes, and green dots for all your aunts' and uncles' homes.

"X" Marks the spot where you live.

SPECIAL OCCASION
CELEBRATIONS, FAMILY REUNIONS
AND GET-TOGETHERS

Some families try to get everyone
together to celebrate things like
weddings, births and religious holidays.
When does your family try to get
together? For what occasions?

How about your birthday? How does
your family celebrate birthdays?

What are some of your family's
customs for other special occasions?

Has your family ever had a family
reunion? When? Where? How many
people were there? Who did you meet?

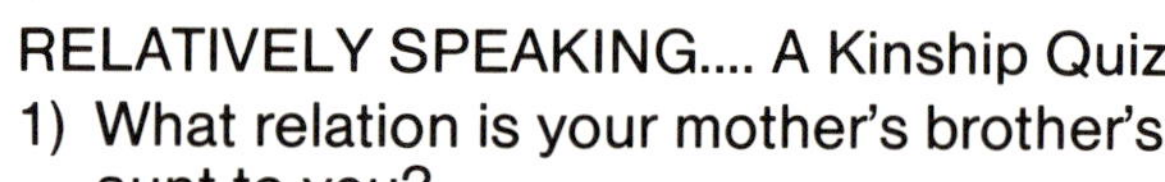

RELATIVELY SPEAKING.... A Kinship Quiz
1) What relation is your mother's brother's father's
   aunt to you?
2) How about your sister's father's brother's
   daughter?
3) Who is your uncle's brother?
4) Or, your father's father's grandchild?
5) Who is your cousins's mother's sister?

AND CELEBRATIONS

Draw a picture of a family special occasion the way your family celebrates it.

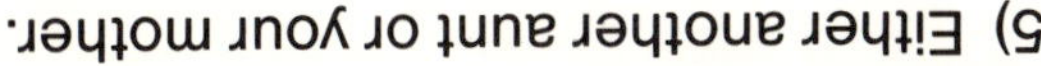

Quiz Answers:
1) Your great-great aunt.
2) Your cousin.
3) Either your father or another uncle.
4) That's YOU!
5) Either another aunt or your mother.

ENOUGH FAMILY! Let's get back to something a little closer to home. Let's do some more about ME! Right now, these are my favorites: (List some of your favorite things, such as cartoon, best friend, movie, joke, musical group, or toy.)

____
____
____
____
____
____
____
____

Draw some pictures of your favorite things in the space provided and color them your favorite colors.

If you have a pet, draw him or her here, or stick in a photograph. If you don't have a pet, draw a picture of one you've always wanted. What's your pet's name? _______ What is he or she?_______ ___________ How old is he or she? _________ What you like best about your pet:_____

____

Draw a picture here of a hero you may have, someone you respect and admire. OR draw a picture of what you want to be when you grow up, like a doctor or an astronaut.

MORE RELATED FACTS:

I started school when I was __________ years old. That was in 19 ______. Right now I go to (name of school) __________ __________________, which is located at: (address) __________________ __________________

I'm in Grade__________. My teacher's name is__________________
The principal's name is ______________ __________________

My favorite subject is __________________ __________________

My least favorite subject is __________ __________________

If you have no pet, write down here what you'd like to have and why.

____
____
____

Do you have an imaginary friend? Is he or she a person or a thing or an animal? __________________
Does he or she come from another planet? __________________
What's he or she like?__________________
____
What things do you do together?

____
____

Could you draw a picture of your imaginary friend? Try. Draw your picture here.

RELEVANT RELATIVES, a relatively simple trivia quiz

1) Who was Jor-El's super son?

2) "Kitty Hawk" was the name of their plane, who were the famous brothers who flew it?

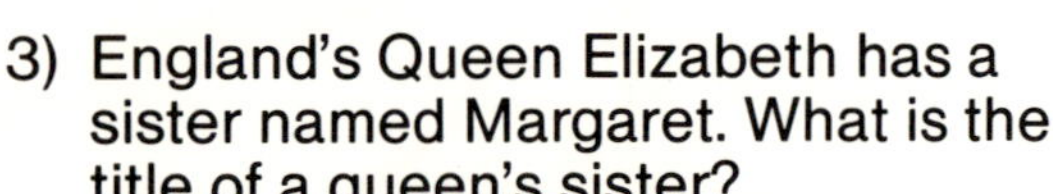

3) England's Queen Elizabeth has a sister named Margaret. What is the title of a queen's sister?

4) Who was Little Red Riding Hood going to visit?

5) Who is Captain Stubing's daughter?

6) The Wicked Witch of the West had a sister. Who was she and what happened to her?

7) Name Tom Sawyer's aunt.

8) In the Charles M. Shultz comic strip, who is Lucy's brother? What is their last name?

9) This famous lady goose tells nursery rhymes. Who is she?

10) This famous royal couple had a baby. What is the baby's name? What are his parents' names?

11) Can you name all three of Donald Duck's nephews?

12) Name Dorothy's aunt.

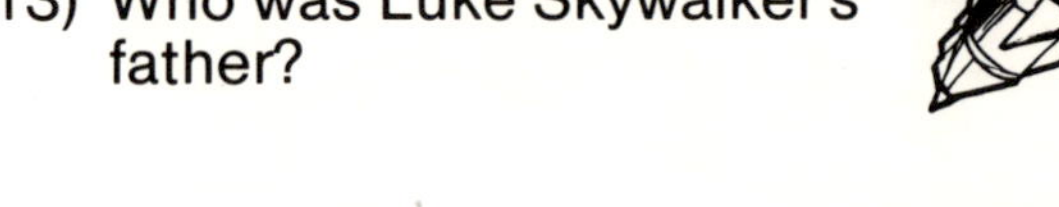

13) Who was Luke Skywalker's father?

14) King Richard's brother was Robin Hood's enemy. Who was he?

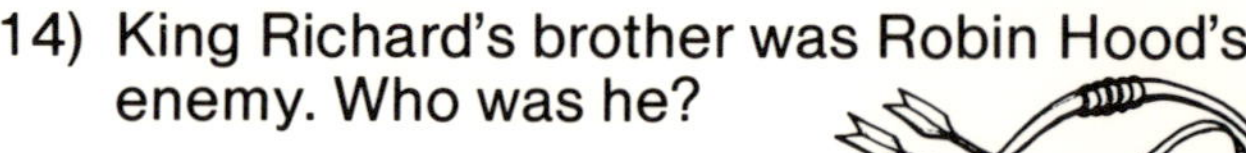

15) Where did Dorothy and E.T. both want to go?

16) In a nursery rhyme a brother and a sister went for a walk in the woods and came across a gingerbread house. Who were they?

17) How are the Dukes of Hazard related?

18) Who is Bobby Ewing's famous television brother?

19) A man and a woman who lived in the jungle had a son they named Boy. Who were they?

20) What famous Daddy wasn't really Orphan Annie's true father?

TRIVIA QUIZ ANSWERS:
1) Superman, 2) Orville and Wilbur Wright, 3) Princess, 4) Her grandmother, 5) Vicki, 6) The Wicked Witch of the East, and Dorothy's house fell on her, 7) Aunt Polly, 8) Linus VanPelt, 9) Mother Goose, 10) William, Charles and Diana, 11) Hewie, Dewie and Louie, 12) Em, 13) Darth Vader, 14) Prince John, 15) Home, 16) Hanzel and Gretel, 17) Luke and Bo are brothers, 18) J.R., 19) Tarzan and Jane, 20) Daddy Warbucks.

FOR MORE INFORMATION...

Everyone is curious about his or her family. This book may have only sparked your interest and you may want to go on and find out more about your family, many more generations past. Where should you start to look for things and what should you look for?

First of all, you'll find that as you go back into the past, there are fewer and fewer photographs and personal belongings left behind and you'll notice more and more of your information is coming from old records and other written documents. These are the types of things you start looking for. Certificates of birth, death and marriages can give you lots of information. So can other types of records, like religious records. Old legal documents can tell you what your relations were doing, say, 100 years ago; did they buy a house or write a will?

The very best place to start your search is in your public library. The librarian can see what you've got and help you discover where you should be heading.

Investigate various spellings of your last name. Remember, it wasn't very long ago that not everyone could read and write, and those who could weren't very good at it. If your name is "Smith" you might be related to a "Smythe" family somewhere!

Interview as many of your relatives as you can first, then go in search of supporting documentation for the things you've learned. One piece of information is usually also a clue to finding another. Always keep a record of your sources and keep photocopies of any paperwork you come up with.

Good hunting!

Stick an envelope here
to hold your extra photos or
drawings.